ANIMAL CLASSES
Birds

by Kari Schuetz

BELLWETHER MEDIA • MINNEAPOLIS, MN

Note to Librarians, Teachers, and Parents:

Blastoff! Readers are carefully developed by literacy experts and combine standards-based content with developmentally appropriate text.

Level 1 provides the most support through repetition of high-frequency words, light text, predictable sentence patterns, and strong visual support.

Level 2 offers early readers a bit more challenge through varied simple sentences, increased text load, and less repetition of high-frequency words.

Level 3 advances early-fluent readers toward fluency through increased text and concept load, less reliance on visuals, longer sentences, and more literary language.

Level 4 builds reading stamina by providing more text per page, increased use of punctuation, greater variation in sentence patterns, and increasingly challenging vocabulary.

Level 5 encourages children to move from "learning to read" to "reading to learn" by providing even more text, varied writing styles, and less familiar topics.

Whichever book is right for your reader, Blastoff! Readers are the perfect books to build confidence and encourage a love of reading that will last a lifetime!

This edition first published in 2013 by Bellwether Media, Inc.

No part of this publication may be reproduced in whole or in part without written permission of the publisher. For information regarding permission, write to Bellwether Media, Inc., Attention: Permissions Department, 5357 Penn Avenue South, Minneapolis, MN 55419.

Library of Congress Cataloging-in-Publication Data
Schuetz, Kari.
  Birds / by Kari Schuetz.
      p. cm. – (Blastoff! readers: animal classes)
  Includes bibliographical references and index.
  Summary: "Simple text and full-color photography introduce beginning readers to birds. Developed by literacy experts for students in kindergarten through third grade"–Provided by publisher.
  ISBN 978-1-60014-772-2 (hardcover : alk. paper)
  1. Birds–Juvenile literature. I. Title.
  QL676.2.S383 2013
  598–dc23   2011053034

Printed in the United States of America, North Mankato, MN.

Table of Contents

Every animal **species** is one of a kind. However, they are all members of the animal kingdom.

They belong to groups based
on common features.

What Are Birds?

Birds are one of the five main **classes** of **vertebrates**. They are the only class with feathers.

The Animal Kingdom

vertebrates

examples of animals with backbones

amphibians

birds

fish

mammals

reptiles

invertebrates

examples of animals without backbones

arachnids

crustaceans

insects

Birds are **warm-blooded** animals. They keep a constant body temperature.

Soft feathers called **down** keep them warm in cold **climates**.

Birds begin life inside hard, waterproof eggs. Parents **incubate** the eggs as the birds develop inside.

Baby birds hatch from
the eggs. They use
their beaks to break
out of the shells.

Some birds are nearly bald when they hatch. Others are covered with down.

All birds grow adult feathers. They **molt** their feathers once or twice a year.

Not all feathers are used for flight. Some birds move on the ground or in water.

Ostriches can sprint
over 40 miles
(65 kilometers)
per hour on land.
Penguins often glide
through water.

Many birds that fly **migrate** with the seasons. They travel to warm places during cold winter months.

These places offer more hours
of daylight and more food.

Birds can perform amazing feats. The peregrine falcon is the fastest animal in the world.

It dives through the air at 200 miles (322 kilometers) per hour. The quick cheetah could never keep up with this bird!

peregrine falcon

Big-Name Birds

Fastest Running/Largest:
ostrich

Smallest:
bee hummingbird

Longest Wingspan:
wandering albatross

Fastest Swimming:
gentoo penguin

Loudest:
superb lyrebird

Longest Migration:
Arctic tern

Arctic tern

gentoo
penguin

Glossary

classes—groups within the animal kingdom; members of a specific class share many of the same characteristics.

climates—areas with specific temperatures and weather patterns

down—fine feathers that keep birds warm

incubate—to keep warm; most birds sit on their eggs to incubate them until they hatch.

migrate—to move from place to place, often with the seasons

molt—to shed or let fall off; birds molt their feathers every year as new feathers grow.

species—groups of related animals; all animals of a specific species have the same characteristics.

vertebrates—members of the animal kingdom that have backbones

warm-blooded—able to maintain a constant body temperature in both warm and cold climates

To Learn More

AT THE LIBRARY

Burnie, David. *Bird*. New York, N.Y.: DK Pub, Inc., 2008.

Dunphy, Madeleine. *The Peregrine's Journey: A Story of Migration*. Berkeley, Calif.: Web of Life Children's Books, 2008.

Rabe, Tish. *Fine Feathered Friends: All About Birds*. New York, N.Y.: Random House, 1998.

ON THE WEB

Learning more about birds is as easy as 1, 2, 3.

1. Go to www.factsurfer.com.

2. Enter "birds" into the search box.

3. Click the "Surf" button and you will see a list of related Web sites.

With factsurfer.com, finding more information is just a click away.

Index